THE STORY OF GOING-TO-THE-SUN ROAD

WHO BUILT THE ROAD, DADDY?

WRITTEN BY JOYCE SIBLERUD SCHMAUTZ
ILLUSTRATED BY KADYN SCHMAUTZ PAYA

Who built the road, Daddy?
I really want to know.
Did they build it in the rain?
Did they build it in the snow?

Yes, they built it in the rain
and they built it in the snow.
They built it in the sunshine
and when the winds would blow.

How did they move the trees
that stood firmly in their way?
And what about the boulders?
How did they carry them away?

Sometimes they used a cross saw,
sometimes they used an ax.
They stripped the branches and the limbs.
Sometimes it hurt their backs.

Some rocks were moved by levers,
and some were blasted out.
At times the men would carry
the loose rocks down the mount.

How did they get supplies in?

The lumber and the nails?

The shovels, picks, and axes,

to build this marvelous trail?

They brought them in on wagons
sometimes on cars or trucks,
on horseback, mules, or railroad trains,
through rain and snow and muck.

What happened when the wagons got loaded down and stuck?

How did they pull the wagons out when people had bad luck?

The horses pulled the wagons out. Sometimes the men pushed, too.
They pushed and pulled and pulled and pushed 'til they popped out of the goo.

Who cut down the trees?
Who blasted out the stumps?
Did noises scare the animals?
Did rocks scatter and jump?

Young and old men cut the trees
and blasted out the stumps.
The noises scared the animals
they made the critters jump!

Where were the bears and mountain goats?
Did they watch the men?
Did the workers watch the wild ones
or chase them to their dens?

Yes, the bears and mountain goats
were curious about the men.
The workers watched the wild ones
and chased them to their dens.

Where did the workers sleep at night? Just where did they lay?

Did they sleep in tents or cabins or did they sleep in hay?

The workers slept in tents all lined up in a camp.

Sometimes it was hot and dry and sometimes cold and damp.

Who cooked the food that fed them?
Where did they get their lunch?
How did they cook so many things
to feed that hungry bunch?

Men and women were the cooks
who fed that hungry bunch.
Biscuits, bacon, and sandwiches
were what they made for lunch.

The men who built were brave ones
a fine and hearty crew.
Many came, some gave their all
'til the work on the road was through.

They call it "Going-to-the-Sun."
It reaches toward the sky.
At Logan Pass, the very top,
it's more than a mile high.

I am so glad they built the road
so we can drive and see
the wonders of the mountains,
the rivers, and the trees.

So here's to all the workers who worked in rain and snow.

Here's to all the brave ones who built this mighty road.

Glacier's Going-to-the-Sun Road

"We may confidently declare that there is no highway which will give the sightseer, the lover of grandeur of the Creator's handiwork, more thrills, more genuine satisfaction deep down in his being than will a trip over this road."

– Frank Cooney, Montana Governor, July 15, 1933

The land that is now known as Glacier National Park was frequented by the Blackfeet, Salish, Pend d'Oreille, and Kootenai peoples for many generations before the arrival of white explorers on horseback. After President Taft established Glacier National Park in 1910, plans were begun to make the park's wonders more accessible to visitors, and in 1918 the idea of an automobile route across the park's interior began to take shape.

Over the next fifteen years, crews from all over the United States from diverse backgrounds and nationalities worked to move tons of excavated rock and grade the roadway for safe travel. Crews did back-breaking work in all weather and in the company of curious wildlife, all while living in tent camps along the construction route.

The first car drove over Going-to-the-Sun-Road, officially named for the nearby Going-to-the-Sun Mountain, in the fall of 1932. A grand opening ceremony was held on Logan Pass, the highest point on the road at 6,646 feet, on July 15, 1933. More than 4,000 people, including dignitaries and some of the many workers, were present for the opening. The work of transitioning the gravel road to asphalt pavement would continue until 1952, and maintenance and construction is an ongoing project in the twenty-first century.

By Kadyn Schmautz Paya

The authors gratefully acknowledge C.W. Guthrie's books, Glacier National Park: The First Hundred Years *and* Going-to-the-Sun Road: Glacier National Park's Highway to the Sky *as sources for this book. For more information about Going-to-the-Sun Road, readers can also visit the Glacier National Park page at www.nps.gov.*

Gunsight Pass Trail, Glacier National Park

About the Author & Illustrator

Joyce Siblerud Schmautz is a third-generation Montanan raised on the same farm as her father (and her uncles, to whom this book is dedicated) in Kalispell, Montana.

Her daughter, Kadyn Schmautz Paya, was raised in Kalispell and has worked around Glacier National Park for several seasons, including as a park ranger.

They have enjoyed many hikes together and consider Glacier National Park a favorite place. This is their first book.

FOR HAROLD AND MAYNARD SIBLERUD
WHO HELPED BUILD THE ROAD.

TO GOD BE THE GLORY.

ISBN: 978-1-56037-801-3

Text by Joyce Siblerud Schmautz
Illustration by Kadyn Schmautz Paya

For more information about our books, write Farcountry Press, P.O. Box 5630, Helena, MT 59604; call (800) 821-3874; or visit www.farcountrypress.com.

Produced in the United States of America.
Printed in Canada.

25 24 23 22 21 1 2 3 4 5 6